BABEL

Story by
Marc Lumer
Chaim Burston
DouBer Naiditch

Art by
Marc Lumer

Once the world was young,
like a little child.

And the lion, the lamb, the birds, the
butterflies, and the people living in it
were young, too.

They all lived together
in a beautiful valley,
and they all spoke to each other
in one beautiful language,
a language God had given them.

But the people grew and multiplied.
And soon the beautiful valley got
very crowded.

There was no longer enough room for a man or a woman or their children, not even for their little lamb.

So the men and women, boys and girls took everything they had and found a new valley, a bigger valley, to call home.

And in their single language they said to each other, "We will make a great city here, and call it Babel. And we will live in Babel together, with our children and our children's children."

"And in its center, like a mountain,
we'll build a tower bigger than any building,
bigger even than the great mountains
that God has made!"

Together all the people worked as one to build the greatest and tallest tower that ever was.

And because the nation was so young,
they still remembered when God broke the sky
and filled the world with water for forty days and nights.

They thought that their tower would hold up the sky and stay above the waters. They even thought they would no longer need God. "The tower will keep us safe!" they said.

So mothers and fathers made the tower their work.

And children made the tower their home.

They wore tower hats.

They ate tower cakes.

They sang tower songs and drew tower pictures.

They played tower games with tower pieces.

And dreamt dreams of a tower taller than the sky.

And the people said to themselves in their single language, "How great we are! We've built a tower so tall that even God can't wash it away!"

They grew so proud that they tried to build the tower even higher, so high that they could make war with God! Then they'd take the heavens as their home.

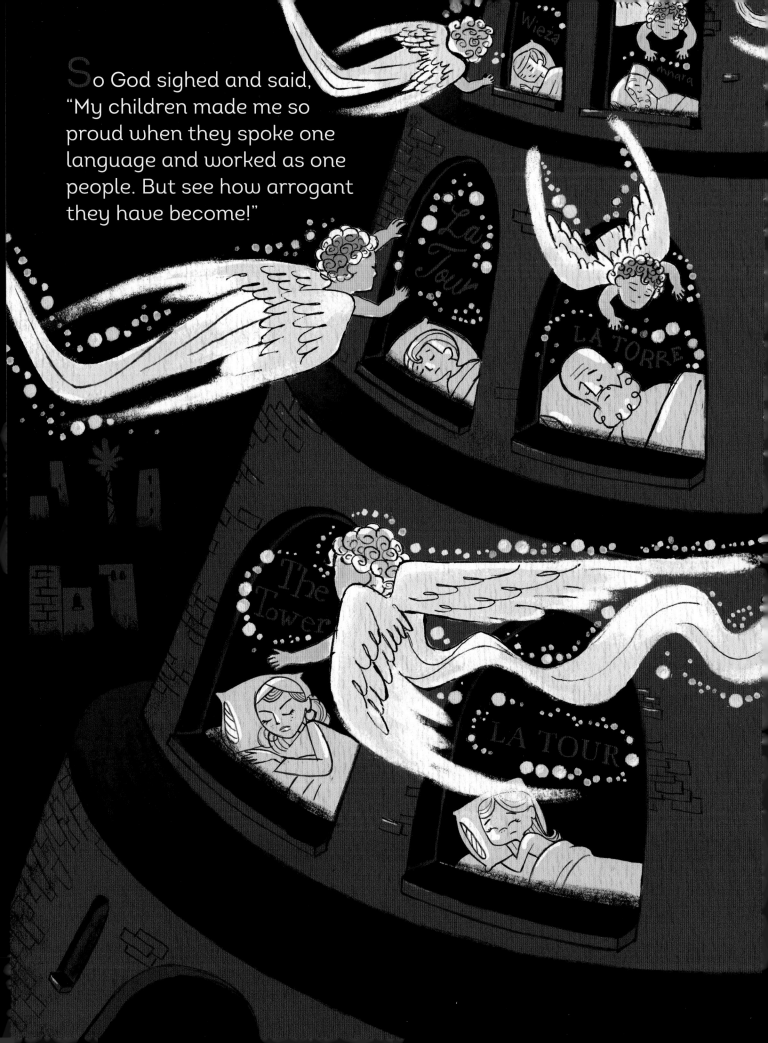

So God sighed and said, "My children made me so proud when they spoke one language and worked as one people. But see how arrogant they have become!"

And while they slept, God sent angels to erase the old language from their heads and leave in its place a new and different language for each one of them.

The next day, there was terrible confusion. Joseph woke up as José, and Jacob was Jacques, and when one asked the other for bread, he got a harder loaf than he expected!

With their one language, they had become great, but so arrogant they thought they could hold up the sky with a tower!

But with many languages, they could not even agree on what to call the tower, or the sky, and they remembered that they were small and the world was so very big.

With new words.

To my parents, Gunter & Linda Lumer ע״ה, and my son Benny.
Special thanks to my talented assistant, Miri Rooney. -M.L.

For all who survive their flood, leave their ark, and make the world a better place. -C.B.

To my amazing wife, and to my many sweet children. -D.B.N.

Design by Marc Lumer
Edited by Ann D. Koffsky

———

Apples & Honey Press
An imprint of Behrman House and Gefen Publishing House
Behrman House, 11 Edison Place, Springfield, NJ 07081
Gefen Publishing House Ltd, 6 Hatzvi Street, Jerusalem 94386, Israel
www.applesandhoneypress.com

Text copyright © 2016 by Marc Lumer, Chaim Burston, and DovBer Naiditch
Illustrations copyright © 2016 by Marc Lumer

ISBN 978-1-68115-514-2

Library of Congress Cataloging-in-Publication Data
Lumer, Marc, author.
Babel / by Marc Lumer, Chaim Burston, and Dov Naiditch; illustrations by Marc Lumer.

pages cm

1. Babel, Tower of--Juvenile literature. 2. Bible stories, English--Genesis--Juvenile literature.
I. Burston, Chaim, co-author. II. Naiditch, Dov, co-author. III. Lumer, Marc, illustrator. IV. Title.
BS1238.B2L86 2016 222'.1109505--dc23 2015026960
Printed in the United States
1 3 5 7 9 8 6 4 2